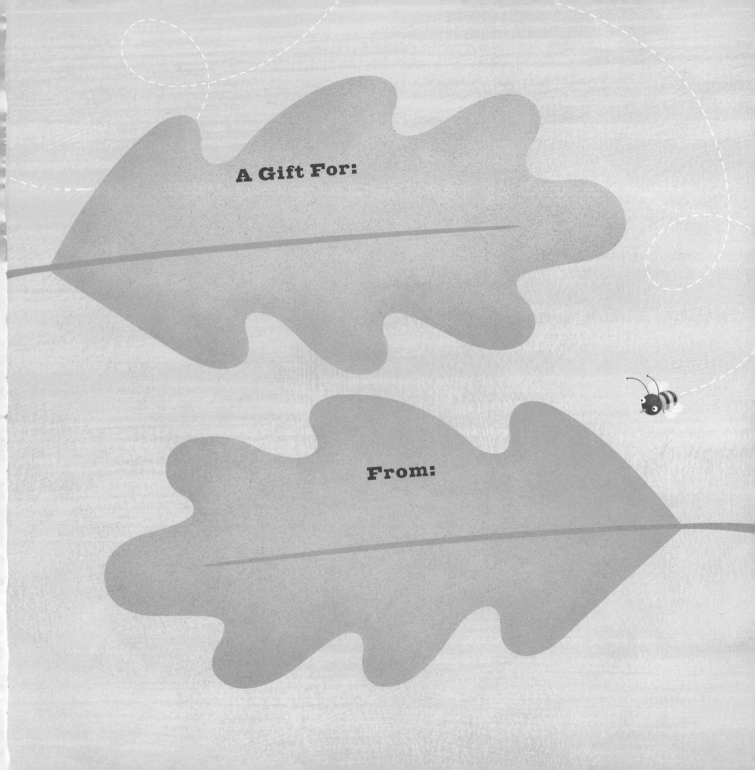

A Gift For:

From:

How to Use Your Interactive Storybook & Story Buddy:

1. Press your Story Buddy's ear to start.
2. Read the story aloud in a quiet place. Speak in a clear voice when you see the highlighted phrases.
3. Listen to your buddy respond with several different phrases throughout the book.

Clarity and speed of reading affect Watson's response. He may not always respond to young children.

Watch for even more Interactive Storybooks and Story Buddies. Available only at Hallmark. For more information, visit us on the Web at www.Hallmark.com/StoryBuddy.

Copyright © 2011 Hallmark Licensing, Inc.

Published by Hallmark Books,
a division of Hallmark Cards, Inc.,
Kansas City, MO 64141
Visit us on the Web at www.Hallmark.com.

Editors: Emily Osborn and Megan Langford
Art Director: Kevin Swanson
Designer: Mary Eakin
Production Artist: Dan Horton

ISBN: 978-1-59530-355-4
KOB8003
Printed and bound in China
OCT10

BOOK 2

Watson and the Case of
The Missing Acorn

By **Katherine Stano** | Illustrated by **Karla Taylor**

Hallmark
GIFT BOOKS

One sunny spring day, a clever raccoon named Watson wandered through the forest. He had lots of things to figure out. He wondered why the bees buzzed and the birds chirped. He wondered why the sun winked at him through the tall trees.

Yes, Watson loved solving mysteries.

Watson was very good at figuring things out. Once he even figured out that blueberries turned his tongue bright blue! All his forest friends thought Watson was a discovery genius! Soon he became the go-to raccoon for every woodland mystery that needed to be solved.

One day, he heard a rowdy rustling in the woods.
"Wowza! What is that?" thought the clever raccoon.
Suddenly, he heard a cry for help.
"Watson! Somebody call Watson!"

Before Watson could even grab his trusty mystery-
solving gear, his friend Earl Squirrel popped in.
"Watson, I could really use your help!"

Watson was all ears as Earl explained his puzzling problem. "I can't find my... oh, what's the name of that silly thing... acorn! That's it! Acorn!" the squirrel hollered. "It's gone! It disappeared! It vanished before my very bright eyes!"

Watson grinned. He knew right where
it was. With super speed, Watson dashed
to his den, snatched a bright yellow cob
of corn, and flung it to Earl Squirrel.

"You must have left it here the other day. Mystery solved!" said Watson. The more cases he worked, the more Watson loved solving mysteries.

Though the snack sounded delicious, Earl
shook his head. "No. Not corn! An ACORN! A nut!
My favorite nut!" he said. "Please, Watson,
we must find my acorn!"

Earl Squirrel led Watson to a nearby clearing.
"I dug a hole, uh, somewhere around here," said Earl.
"I buried it right under a little pile of dirt to keep it safe."
Watson studied the area. Yes, the nut was indeed
missing. There was only a mysterious green sprout
popping up from the rich spring dirt.

Watson knew he had work to do. "How did you find this very important nut?" he asked.

"I was practicing my tree-leaping skills, when out of nowhere, bobbling on a limb, I saw it—the sweetest, neatest nut in the world. Oh, Watson, we must find my acorn!"

"When did you last see this missing nut?" Watson asked his frantic friend.

Earl Squirrel furrowed his eyebrows. "It was a drizzly day. Rain plopped and dropped from the clouds. The trees were colorful, like apples and oranges and bananas."

"Yum! I sure do love bananas," Watson said with a hungry grin. But this was no time for a snack.

Quickly, Watson declared, "I'm calling
for a search party!" But before he could say
another word, some cheerful chipmunks rushed
to the scene.

"Search party? Did someone say 'search
party'?" they squeaked. "We'll help you. Watson,
we believe in you!"

And so they began to search. They searched high. They searched low. They searched big places. They searched teeny-tiny places. They even questioned the locals.

They searched all day. And still no nut.

Watson started to wonder if he'd ever find Earl Squirrel's hidden treasure. He'd solved a lot of mysteries in his time, but this was one tough nut to crack!

Just as he was about to lose hope, the chipmunks boosted his spirits. "Don't give up! Watson, we believe in you!"

Just then, Ollie Owl flew over-head. Watson knew she'd be able to help. Ollie Owl had smarts!

As the bird perched, Watson explained the whole troublesome tale. She listened sharply, then said, "This sprout is clearly a very tiny tree. You know, if you plant an acorn, it will grow into a grand oak tree."

Suddenly, it all made sense. This little green sprout **WAS** the acorn that Earl Squirrel had buried. And someday, the sprout would become a huge tree with more acorns than Earl would know what to do with. Thanks to Ollie Owl, Watson had cracked the case.

"Hooray for Watson!" cried Earl as the chipmunks applauded.

The little raccoon beamed. Oh, how Watson loved solving mysteries!

Did you have fun solving
this mystery with Watson?
Tell us about it!

Please send your comments to:
Hallmark Book Feedback
P.O. Box 419034
Mail Drop 215
Kansas City, MO 64141

Or e-mail us at:
booknotes@hallmark.com